Pat Summitt™

Accomplishments

- In 38 seasons, Pat Summitt coached 161 players at the University of Tennessee
- 100% student-athlete graduation rate
- 8 National Championships
- 18 NCAA "Final Fours"
- Never missed a NCAA tournament appearance
- 32 SEC Championships
- 15 "Coach of the Year" Awards
- Awarded 9 Medals for coaching the U.S. National Team
- Founded the Pat Summitt Foundation
- Member of U.S. Department of State's Council to Empower Women & Girls Through Sports
- Only person to win Olympic medals as both player (1976) and head coach (1984)
- 1,098 victories (retired as winningest coach in NCAA history, men or women)
- Awarded the Winged Foot Award from the New York Athletic Club for coaches reaching the highest levels in coaching
- Wrote three New York Times Best Seller books

Awards Named After Pat

NCAA Pat Summitt Award
USBWA Pat Summitt Most Courageous Award
ESPNW Pat Summitt Coaching Award
WBCA The Pat Summitt Trophy
Tennessee Hall of Fame Pat Summitt Lifetime Achievement Award

Quotes from the

Summitt

Quotes from the

Summitt

by Pat Summitt
"Coach of the Century"

Pat Summitt™
PUBLISHING

PREMIUM
PRESS
AMERICA

LEADERSHIP GROUP

The Pat Summitt Leadership Group inspires through film, educational programs, and publishing. We are committed to improving the personal and professional lives of young girls and women by providing important information from time-tested ' lessons derived from the life, legacy and wisdom of the iconic coach Pat Summitt.

Quotes from the Summitt by Pat Summitt

© 2019 Pat Summitt Leadership Group*

Published by
Pat Summitt Publishing/Premium Press America, Nashville, Tennessee

ISBN 978-1-933725-56-7
Library of Congress Catalog Card Number 2018957596

Pat Summitt Publishing books are available at special discounts for premiums, promotions, fundraising, sales, or educational use. For details or to order books contact The Publisher, P.O. Box 58995, Nashville, TN 37205; call 615-353-7902; or email orders@premiumpressamerica.com

Text and cover design: 828Marketing.com, Nashville, Tennessee

Photographs are provided courtesy of the University of Tennessee and the Summitt family, Tom Raymond, www.freshairphoto.com, Patrick Murphy-Racey, www.pmrphoto.com and Knoxville News Sentinel.

Printed in the United States of America
1 2 3 4 5 6 7 8 9 10

*To learn more about the Pat Summitt Leadership Group
go to www.PatSummittLeadershipGroup.com

Dedication

Although an iconic,
history-making basketball coach,
Pat Summitt viewed herself
as a teacher and educator first.
It is precisely her penchant for
offering profound advice,
words of wisdom and instruction
that serves as the foundation for
Quotes from the Summitt, which is dedicated
to those individuals who discipline themselves
to become their very best... Pat Summitt style.

Acknowledgments

The Pat Summitt Leadership Group is grateful for contributions,
support, hard work and commitment put forth
to compile this book of wisdom from the
American treasure, Coach Pat Summitt.

Sincere appreciation goes out to Ryan Blumenthal
for his tireless work compiling hundreds of quotations and photos.
We also extend our thanks to Brooklyn Summitt and Jordan Pumroy
for research assistance, George and Bette Schnitzer of
Premium Press America for their publishing wisdom
and leadership and of course the University of Tennessee
for opening up their archives to us and giving us permission
to use many of the historical photos found in this book.

We also acknowledge the insight and never-ending support
from Tyler Summitt, Pat Summitt's son, who has dedicated himself
toward keeping his Mom's legacy and words of wisdom alive.

Introduction

Quotes from the Summitt is an empowering collection of quotations Pat used to help mold and energize her players. This book is a must read for people of all ages and in all walks of life. Readers will not only learn from Pat's profound insights but also become challenged to act on many of the quotations inasmuch as each quote is focused on growth, improvement, success and fulfillment.

Pat was a person who never let the opportunity to educate and inspire others pass. **Words of wisdom in this book, many written in her own handwriting, represent quotes Pat readily used.** She was a born educator and always dared and cared to share ideas, information, insights and counsel in hopes of making a difference and providing everyone she met with value. It was precisely her caring to educate and inspire that is the foundation of this wonderful compilation of quotations.

This book demonstrates how much Pat Summitt cared at all levels to help people, especially women, to achieve their life goals. As Pat would often say, *"Nobody cares how much you know until they know how much you care."*

Quotes from the Summitt is consistent with the Pat Summitt Leadership Group's focus on educating and inspiring individuals through the timeless principles for success and leadership in business and in life established by Pat Summitt.

On behalf of my colleagues, we are excited you're about to experience the wisdom of an American treasure. Enjoy this book, learn from it and pass it along to someone you care about. After all, it's all about showing how much you care.

Kimberly Lain Blumenthal, President
Pat Summitt Leadership Group

Foreword

by Mickie DeMoss
2018 Women's Basketball Hall of Fame Inductee

In 2018, when I was humbled and honored by being inducted into the Women's Basketball Hall of Fame, I gave thanks to a number of people who were instrumental in my life and who served as my role-models and sources of inspiration. On stage, I shared with the audience of over 1,000 people that my single most important acknowledgment was my tribute to Pat Summitt, my mentor and friend. I proudly served as Pat Summitt's Assistant Head Coach 20 years at the University of Tennessee. We won 16 SEC Championships, had 13 Final Four appearances and won 6 NCAA National Championships together. It was some of the best times of my life.

Pat Summitt was truly an American treasure. She was an iconic women's basketball coach who was named "Coach of the Century." When Sporting News Magazine named the "Top 100 Greatest Coaches of All Time in All Sports in the U.S.," Pat Summitt was the only woman on the list. Yes, she was a champion for gender equality, a trailblazer for women, and a stellar educator who in 38 years of coaching saw 100% of her student-athletes graduate college. She was a three-time New York Times best-selling author, a prolific public speaker and named by the White House as "Top 25 Most Influential Working Mothers." Her achievements, milestones and accolades would fill the pages of this book and more.

DeMoss and Summitt, photo by Tom Raymond, Fresh Air Photo

Coach Summitt was also an amazing friend who was always available to lending a helping hand and to provide her sage wisdom and profound counsel. It is precisely Pat Summitt's words of wisdom that makes this book so very special. In this publication, ***Quotes from the Summitt,*** readers will learn, first hand, Coach Summitt's championship philosophies, beliefs, ideals, points of view and insight about sport, yes, but more importantly, about life.

Although many of the quotes in this book might be new to you, I heard Pat use them many, many times in our 30+ years together as friends and colleagues. They are philosophical. They are rich. They are important. Her words are pearls of wisdom that can help change and enhance your life to bring you the success you desire.

Pat Summitt

RESPECT YOURSELF AND OTHERS

TAKE FULL RESPONSIBILITY

HANDLE SUCCESS LIKE YOU HANDLE FAILURE

DEVELOP AND DEMONSTRATE LOYALTY

CHANGE IS A MUST

THE DEFINITE DOZEN

12

BY PAT SUMMITT

LEARN TO BE A GREAT COMMUNICATOR

BE A COMPETITOR

DISCIPLINE YOURSELF SO NO ONE ELSE HAS TO

MAKE WINNING AN ATTITUDE

PUT THE TEAM BEFORE YOURSELF

DON'T JUST WORK HARD, WORK SMART

MAKE HARD WORK YOUR PASSION

—Pat Summitt created The Definite Dozen to highlight her 12 "must have" values for success.

Pat Summitt™

The Definite Dozen is ultimately about paying attention to basics, those things that enable you to achieve a larger, more profound goal.

Pat Summitt™

You have to
discipline yourself
to do something
the right way until
it's second nature.

Pat Summitt

Could you work for you?
Would you enjoy it?

▲▲

Left foot.
Right foot.
Breathe.

▲▲

When a player makes a mistake,
you always want to put them back
in quickly—you don't just berate them
and sit them down with no chance
of redemption.

It's your business to communicate.

Out-work your competition.

Have a plan and work it.

Attitude lies somewhere between emotion and logic. It's that curious mix of optimism and determination that enables you to maintain a positive outlook and to continue plodding in the face of the most adverse circumstances.

Pat Summitt

Live each day with passion.

▲▲

Respect yourself and others.
Respect the game.
Respect your teammates.
Respect your coaches
and be on time.

COACH 1974-2012
D 1098-208

▲▲

Winning doesn't make you better
than anyone.

Listen, gather feedback,
and then execute on it.

If you don't know whose job it is,
it's yours.

God doesn't take things away to be cruel.
He takes things away to make room for
other things. He takes things away
to lighten us. He takes things away
so we can fly.

Pat Summitt

THE DEFINITE DOZEN

12

BY PAT SUMMITT

- RESPECT YOURSELF AND OTHERS
- TAKE FULL RESPONSIBILITY
- DEVELOP AND DEMONSTRATE LOYALTY
- LEARN TO BE A GREAT COMMUNICATOR
- DISCIPLINE YOURSELF SO NO ONE ELSE HAS TO
- MAKE HARD WORK YOUR PASSION
- DON'T JUST WORK HARD, WORK SMART
- PUT THE TEAM BEFORE YOURSELF
- MAKE WINNING AN ATTITUDE
- BE A COMPETITOR
- CHANGE IS A MUST
- HANDLE SUCCESS LIKE YOU HANDLE FAILURE

Respect yourself and others.

Pat Summitt

If you really want to
get something across,
body language, facial
expression, eye contact,
and listening
are all necessary parts
of communicating.

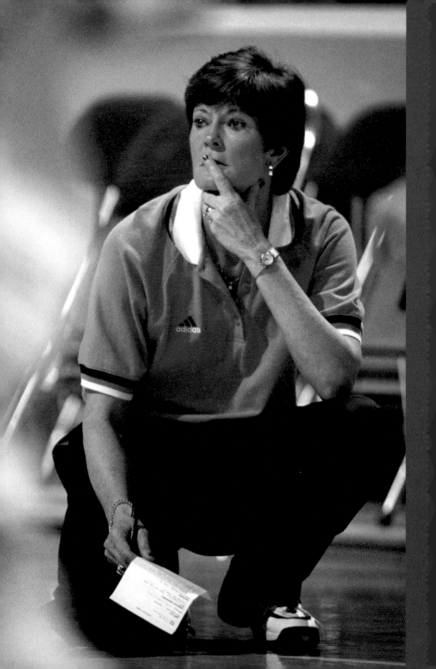

Pat Summitt

It goes fast, so have the right attitude,
work ethic and know-how to
take care of yourself.

Change equals self-improvement.
Push yourself to places you
haven't been before.

I've learned life is tough,
but I am tougher.

You can choose to give your time,
talents and treasures.

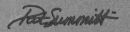

Responsibility is a building block
in both personal and team growth.

If you don't want to
deal with problems,
don't accept the job.

There is a lot more to communicating
than just plain talking.

Pat Summitt

If we didn't have the problem, we wouldn't need the rule. There's a word for that. It's called accountability, and it is the backbone of discipline. You don't have one w without the other.

Pat Summitt

RESPECT YOURSELF AND OTHERS

TAKE FULL RESPONSIBILITY

HANDLE SUCCESS LIKE YOU HANDLE FAILURE

DEVELOP AND DEMONSTRATE LOYALTY

CHANGE IS A MUST

THE DEFINITE DOZEN

12

BY PAT SUMMITT

LEARN TO BE A GREAT COMMUNICATOR

BE A COMPETITOR

DISCIPLINE YOURSELF SO NO ONE ELSE HAS TO

MAKE WINNING AN ATTITUDE

PUT THE TEAM BEFORE YOURSELF

MAKE HARD WORK YOUR PASSION

DON'T JUST WORK HARD, WORK SMART

Take full responsibility.

Pat Summitt

Clear communication
on what will occur
instills confidence in
the performers before the
lights ever
come on.

I wouldn't speak to a player in my office
the same way I would on the court.
Circumstances dictate how you need
to speak, or whether you need
to just shut up and listen.

Sometimes, saying nothing at all
can be just as powerful.

There is always someone better
than you. Whatever it is that you
do for a living, chances are,
you will run into a situation in which
you are not as talented as the person
next to you. That's when being a
competitor can make a difference
in your fortunes.

I've learned the easiest way
to grow as a person is to
surround myself with
people smarter than I am.

Being kind is more important
than being right.

Discipline gets us out of bed
and drives us to be the very best.

Pat Summitt

We want people that take
a lot of pride in being
a part of our program.

▲

Attitude is, in fact, a simple
daily choice. It makes a significant
difference in individual
and group success.

▲

Are you a problem solver
or a problem?

Pat Summitt™

A clear understanding
of what's expected
of each person is crucial.

Loyalty and trust are valuable.

Know your strengths,
weaknesses, and needs.

Be clear on what you want
to say, and say it in a way that
is appropriate to your surroundings.
Too much of one thing tends
to dull your listener's sensibilities.

Pat Summitt

Without an incentive,
people simply wont
work together consistently.
But if you can grasp
the real incentive behind
teamwork, instilling it
suddenly becomes
a whole lot easier.

Pat Summitt™

Confidence is what
happens when you're
done the hard work
that entitles you
to succeed.

If you don't want responsibility,
don't sit in the big chair.
That's the deal.
To be successful,
you must accept
full responsibility.

You have to listen,
to develop effective,
meaningful relationships
with people.

Losing doesn't make you a
bad person.

Pat Summitt

If you don't like your role,
change your performance
and then you'll change your role.

▲▲

*Discipline is the
internal mechanism
that self-motivates you.*

▲▲

I learned when you grow up
on a dairy farm,
cows do not take days off.

Disciplined people
finish the job.

Take care of people
who take care of you.

Praise before you criticize.

Take risks. I once heard
you can't steal second base
with your foot on first.

Discipline is about belief.

It's not enough to say,
"I'm confident."
You can say the words 100 times over,
and no one will buy it
if your shoulders are slumped
and your voice cracks.
You have to project it,
particularly when it comes time
to persuade others.

In pressure situations,
you shouldn't wonder
how your teammate next to you
will react. You should know.

I've learned that everyone wants to live on top of the mountain, but all the happiness and growth occurs while you're climbing it.

Pat and her mom celebrate the renaming of Lady Vols gym to "The Summitt" in 2005.

Pat Summitt

One of the most impressive attributes of that unbeaten team was that they continued to work hard even when they were winning.

I've learned that sometimes all a person needs is a hand to hold and a heart to understand.

Have a sense of urgency and a sense of humor.

You can't hide on a team.

Pat Summitt™

THE DEFINITE DOZEN®
BY PAT SUMMITT

12

RESPECT YOURSELF AND OTHERS

TAKE FULL RESPONSIBILITY

DEVELOP AND DEMONSTRATE LOYALTY

LEARN TO BE A GREAT COMMUNICATOR

DISCIPLINE YOURSELF SO NO ONE ELSE HAS TO

MAKE HARD WORK YOUR PASSION

DON'T JUST WORK HARD, WORK SMART

PUT THE TEAM BEFORE YOURSELF

MAKE WINNING AN ATTITUDE

BE A COMPETITOR

CHANGE IS A MUST

HANDLE SUCCESS LIKE YOU HANDLE FAILURE

Change is a must.

Pat Summitt

When you choose to
be a competitor you
choose to be a survivor.
When you choose to compete,
you make the
conscious decision to
find out what your real
limits are, not just what
you think they are.

—Peyton Manning's favorite Pat Summitt quote

Pat Summitt

You are in control of your
attitude every day.

I hate losing, but it
motivates me and makes me better!

Some people focus on
getting the best life has to give.
I challenge you to
give life your best!

Pat Summitt

Do not compromise
your principles!

Change equals self-improvement.
Push yourself to places you
haven't been before.

Discipline is a signature of
any successful program.

Have pride in your work.

Pat Summitt

Teamwork allows
common people to
obtain uncommon
results.

Pat Summitt

I care first and foremost about
helping each student-athlete
achieve their personal best
on the court, in the classroom
and in life.

Caring is an important
investment that we make
in others.

I have realized throughout my career,
that it's all about relationships.

Pat Summitt

Success is about having
the right person, in the
right place, at the right time.

When you understand yourself
and those around you,
you are better able to
minimize weaknesses and
maximize strengths.

Talent alone won't win,
teamwork always works!

The most difficult part of
self-discipline is convincing
yourself that it's in your own
best interest. Being disciplined
doesn't always feel good.

Do not be afraid
to take risks, in fact,
have the courage to do so.

It's what you learn
after you know it all
that counts the most.

Pat Summitt

RESPECT YOURSELF AND OTHERS

HANDLE SUCCESS LIKE YOU HANDLE FAILURE

TAKE FULL RESPONSIBILITY

CHANGE IS A MUST

DEVELOP AND DEMONSTRATE LOYALTY

THE DEFINITE DOZEN

12

BY PAT SUMMITT

BE A COMPETITOR

LEARN TO BE A GREAT COMMUNICATOR

MAKE WINNING AN ATTITUDE

DISCIPLINE YOURSELF SO NO ONE ELSE HAS TO

PUT THE TEAM BEFORE YOURSELF

MAKE HARD WORK YOUR PASSION

DON'T JUST WORK HARD, WORK SMART

Handle success like you handle failure.

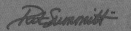

I believe strongly that
you win in life with people.

Adversity will step in your path.
How will you respond?

Don't let anyone outwork you.
Overcome the challenges
and stay the course.

Surround yourself with people of character.

Pat Summitt™

You learn more from losing
than winning.

▲▲

There is no such thing
as self-respect without
respect for others.

▲▲

People who do not respect
those around them will not
make good team members.

Responsibility is a building block
in both personal and team growth.

So, you have a choice.
You can choose to settle for mediocrity,
never venturing forth much effort
or feeling very much.
Or you can commit.
If you commit, I guarantee for
every pain, you will
experience an equal or
surpassing pleasure.

Leadership has been
and will continue to be a key
to the success of any team.

Pat Summitt™

RESPECT YOURSELF AND OTHERS

TAKE FULL RESPONSIBILITY

HANDLE SUCCESS LIKE YOU HANDLE FAILURE

DEVELOP AND DEMONSTRATE LOYALTY

CHANGE IS A MUST

THE DEFINITE DOZEN
12
BY PAT SUMMITT

Make winning an attitude.

BE A COMPETITOR

LEARN TO BE A GREAT COMMUNICATOR

MAKE WINNING AN ATTITUDE

DISCIPLINE YOURSELF SO NO ONE ELSE HAS TO

PUT THE TEAM BEFORE YOURSELF

MAKE HARD WORK YOUR PASSION

DON'T JUST WORK HARD, WORK SMART

Pat Summitt

There is a winner within
each of you. Recognize it!

▲▲

*Find your passion
and never let go of it.*

▲▲

The more responsibility you give
your employees or players,
the more they feel accountable
for the success or failure.

Do whatever it takes
to get the job done.

There is no exact formula for success.

Respect is essential to building
group cohesion.

Nine-tenths of discipline is
having the patience to do things right.

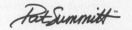

Recognition of consequences
is the sure way to
instill discipline.

Surround yourself with
people who share
the same basic values.

It needs to be 'our' team
and not 'my' team.

You have to have the will
to prepare to win.

Pat Summitt

Competitors aren't afraid to
take risks.

We don't have lazy people
in our organization. They either leave
or I run them off.

Hard work isn't much without
intelligence and understanding.

Pat Summitt

Something I learned from
my father was how bad
you can crave a compliment
if you've never gotten one.
There is this to be said for
a negative reinforcement...
it will motivate you.
I know when I ride my players
how deeply they ache for a good word.

No one feels strong when she examines
her own weakness. But in facing
weakness, you learn how much
there is in you, and you find
real strength.

PatSummitt

I've learned that
love, not time,
heals all wounds.

Pat Summitt

People don't care how
much you know
until they know
how much you care.

The important thing is not about
who is right, but what is right?

You have to set the tone
in your work place.

You have to be a
positive thinker.

Always see the glass half full.
Good Lord... it's morning!
Versus, Good morning, Lord!"

Pat Summitt

Discipline fosters achievement
and self-confidence.

▲▲

Take charge of it
or it will take charge
of you.

▲▲

You can't always control
what happens, but you can
control how you handle it.

Pat Summitt™

RESPECT YOURSELF AND OTHERS

HANDLE SUCCESS LIKE YOU HANDLE FAILURE

TAKE FULL RESPONSIBILITY

CHANGE IS A MUST

DEVELOP AND DEMONSTRATE LOYALTY

THE DEFINITE DOZEN

12

BY PAT SUMMITT

Discipline yourself so no one else has to.

BE A COMPETITOR

LEARN TO BE A GREAT COMMUNICATOR

MAKE WINNING AN ATTITUDE

DISCIPLINE YOURSELF SO NO ONE ELSE HAS TO

PUT THE TEAM BEFORE YOURSELF

MAKE HARD WORK YOUR PASSION

DON'T JUST WORK HARD, WORK SMART

Pat Summitt

There are no shortcuts to success.

*You cant assume
larger responsibility
without taking responsibility
for the small things too.*

Admit to and make yourself
accountable for mistakes.
How can you improve
if you're never wrong?

Pat Summitt

Seek out quality people,
acknowledge their talents,
and let them do their jobs.

▲

Self-discipline is not
the path to instant gratification.
The reward is much farther
down the road, and not
always obvious. But in the end,
it is a much deeper form
of gratification.

▲

The real reward is self-respect
and long-term success.

There are some concrete
ways to create a
winning attitude.
But nothing beats
practicing it. When
you prepare to win,
belief comes easily.

Pat Summitt

Self-discipline is entirely
up to you. You can make
or break your own habits.
No excuses.

Respect is essential to building
group cohesion. People who
do not respect others
will not make good team
members, and they probably
lack self-esteem themselves.

Teamwork is really a form of trust.

Pat Summitt™

RESPECT
YOURSELF
AND
OTHERS

HANDLE
SUCCESS LIKE
YOU HANDLE
FAILURE

TAKE FULL
RESPONSIBILITY

CHANGE
IS A MUST

DEVELOP AND
DEMONSTRATE
LOYALTY

THE DEFINITE DOZEN
12
BY PAT SUMMITT

_Put the team
before yourself._

BE A
COMPETITOR

LEARN TO
BE A GREAT
COMMUNICATOR

MAKE WINNING
AN ATTITUDE

DISCIPLINE
YOURSELF SO
NO ONE ELSE
HAS TO

PUT THE
TEAM BEFORE
YOURSELF

DON'T JUST
WORK HARD,
WORK SMART

MAKE HARD
WORK YOUR
PASSION

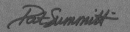
Pat Summitt

If you want to develop loyalty,
the first thing you have to do
is demonstrate it.

Loyalty is a selfless proposition.
You won't ever have it unless you're
willing to give it away first.

Loyalty is not a bargain,
or exchange. It's something
that must be tended to on a
daily basis, and it will be sorely
challenged on occasion.

I've learned that the less time I have to work with, the more things I get done.

Responsibility equals accountability equals ownership. And a sense of ownership, is the most powerful weapon a team or organization can have.

Pat Summitt

People may not always
remember what you say,
but they will remember
how you made them feel.

When you treat others
the way you want to
be treated by being kind,
sincere and genuine, you
demonstrate how much
you really care.

I hire people smarter than me.

Pat Summitt ™ Lady Volunteers

How often do you think
of others before you think
of yourself?

▲▲

Defense has always been
important to me, because
that's something you can control.
Every time you take the floor—
it's how hard you play. It's a
commitment to influence how
your opponents play...because
you don't always have control
as to whether the ball goes
in the basket or not.

Pat Summitt™

Do not compromise your principles!

▲

Role players are critical
to group success.

▲

Plan your work,
and work your plan.

Pat Summitt™

RESPECT YOURSELF AND OTHERS

TAKE FULL RESPONSIBILITY

HANDLE SUCCESS LIKE YOU HANDLE FAILURE

DEVELOP AND DEMONSTRATE LOYALTY

CHANGE IS A MUST

THE DEFINITE DOZEN

12

BY PAT SUMMITT

Learn to be a great communicator.

BE A COMPETITOR

LEARN TO BE A GREAT COMMUNICATOR

MAKE WINNING AN ATTITUDE

DISCIPLINE YOURSELF SO NO ONE ELSE HAS TO

PUT THE TEAM BEFORE YOURSELF

DON'T JUST WORK HARD, WORK SMART

MAKE HARD WORK YOUR PASSION

Listening is crucial to
good communication.

Group discipline produces
a unified effort toward
a common goal.

Self-discipline helps
you believe in yourself.

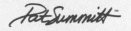

Teamwork doesn't come naturally,
it must be taught.

Discipline helps you finish
a job, and finishing is what
separates excellent work
from average work.

Not everyone can lead.

Pat Summitt

THE DEFINITE DOZEN

12

BY PAT SUMMITT®

RESPECT YOURSELF AND OTHERS

TAKE FULL RESPONSIBILITY

DEVELOP AND DEMONSTRATE LOYALTY

LEARN TO BE A GREAT COMMUNICATOR

DISCIPLINE YOURSELF SO NO ONE ELSE HAS TO

MAKE HARD WORK YOUR PASSION

DON'T JUST WORK HARD, WORK SMART

PUT THE TEAM BEFORE YOURSELF

MAKE WINNING AN ATTITUDE

BE A COMPETITOR

CHANGE IS A MUST

HANDLE SUCCESS LIKE YOU HANDLE FAILURE

Be a competitor.

Pat Summitt

No one ever got anywhere
by being negative.

▲

You can't always be
the most talented person in the room,
but you can be the most competitive.

▲

It's harder to stay on top
than it is to make the climb.
Continue to seek new goals.

Pat Summitt

It is important to love
what you do.

▲

It's important to learn
to laugh at yourself.

▲

I see more in others
than they see in themselves.

Pat Summitt™

You meet the same
people on the way
down that you met
on the way up.

Hard work is about controlling
those things that you are capable
of controlling.

Teamwork is about recognizing
that your personal ambitions and
the ambitions of the team are one
and the same. That's the incentive.

The only effective way to teach
responsibility to younger people
is by making them accountable
to the small things, day in and day out.

Pat Summitt™

Attitude is a choice.
Think positive thoughts daily.

Long-term, repetitive success is
a matter of building a principled
system and sticking to it.
Principles are anchors,
without them you
will drift.

Out work your competition.
Have a plan...work on your plan.

Pat Summitt

If you want to have a great team,
everyone on your team
has to feel important.

▲▲

Sometimes you learn more
from losing than winning.
Losing forces you
to re-evaluate.

▲▲

Change equals self-improvement.
Push yourself to places you
haven't been before.

The future belongs to those who see possibilities before they become obvious.

You can't assume larger responsibility without taking responsibility for the small things too.

Any realistic success formula must include five things: people, system, communication, work ethic, and discipline.

Pat Summitt

Loyalty is not unilateral.
You have to give it to receive it.

▲▲

I've learned that God
doesn't give us everything
we ask for.

▲▲

I've learned under everyone's
hard shell is someone who
wants to be appreciated and loved.

Pat Summitt

Here is how I am going to beat you…
I am going to outwork you.

▲▲

It is what it is.
But it will be
what you make it.

▲▲

The best way to maintain the
credibility of compliments and
criticisms are to use them meaningfully.
Don't overuse them.

When you ask yourself,
'Do I deserve to succeed?'
make sure the answer is yes.

Competition isn't social.
It separates achievers
from the average.

The best way to handle responsibility
is to break it down into smaller parts.
Take care of one small thing at a time.

Pat Summitt

Influence your opponent
by being competitive.
You can affect how your
adversary performs.

◢◣

Combine practice with belief.

◢◣

You can have the brightest,
most creative people in the world,
but if they can't communicate
you won't fully comprehend
what they're capable of.

Pat Summitt

Being responsible sometimes
means making tough,
unpopular decisions.

The family business model
is a successful one because
it fosters loyalty and trust.

Courage, Skill, Perseverance and Will...
are the four leaves of luck's clover;
that we call luck is simply pluck...
and doing things over and over.

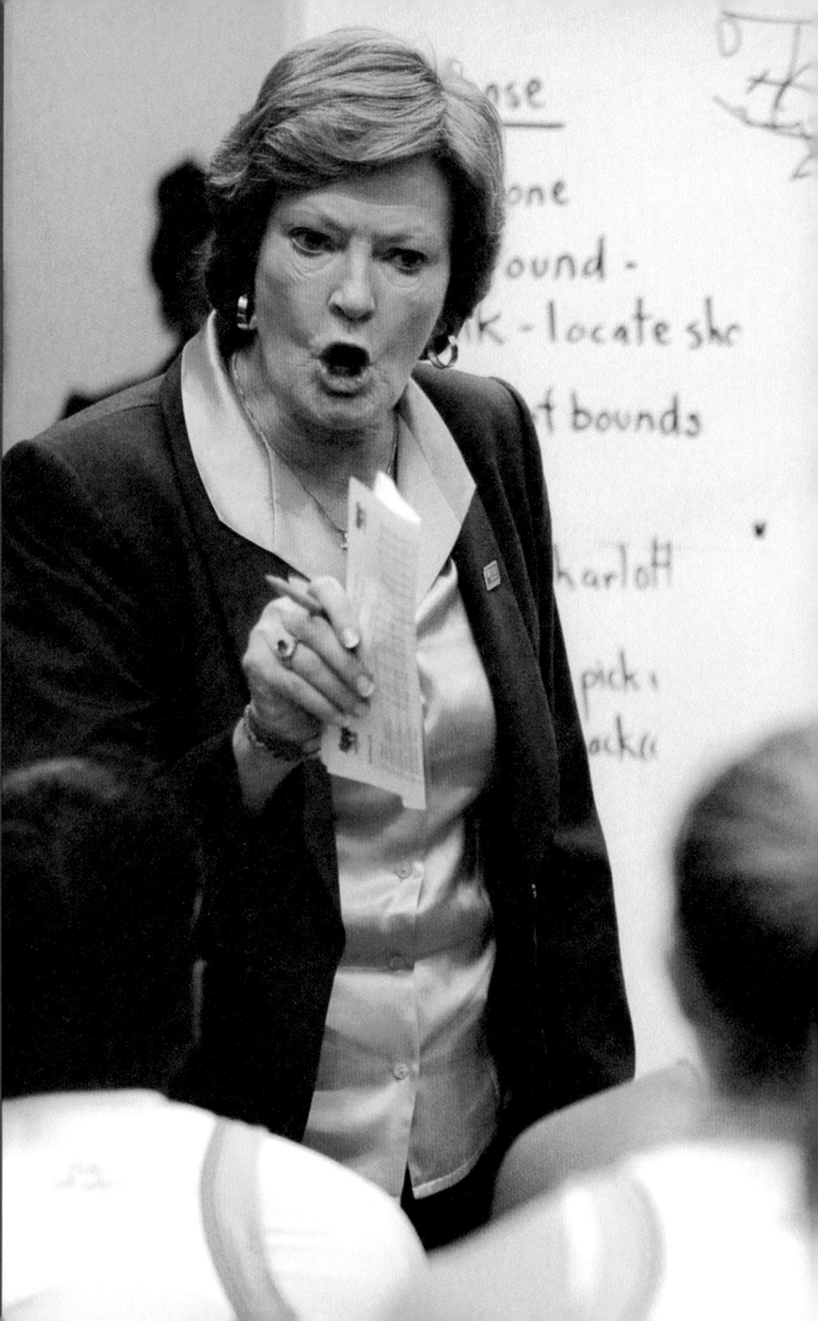

Pat Summitt

ENERGY

You are in control
of your life.
There are four things
you can control every
day of your life:
attitude, work ethic,
how you treat others
and how you treat yourself.

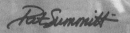

Do the things that aren't fun first,
and do them well.

If I had to describe myself in
one word I would say 'real.'
I'm not trying to be anybody I'm not,
I want people to know who I am.
I hope they understand my passion
and my love for the game
but also about all the people
that have made what's happened
at Tennessee and women's
basketball possible.

You have to have a daily goal,
and you have to make a daily
commitment to the goal.

Be fair, the fewer rules you have
the fewer rules will be broken.
Establishing discipline will be a lot
easier if you don't burden people
with a lot of silly minor regulations.
All you need is a handful of
fair ones that you are prepared
to enforce.

Pat Summitt

Make hard work your passion.

RESPECT YOURSELF AND OTHERS

HANDLE SUCCESS LIKE YOU HANDLE FAILURE

TAKE FULL RESPONSIBILITY

CHANGE IS A MUST

DEVELOP AND DEMONSTRATE LOYALTY

THE DEFINITE DOZEN
12
BY PAT SUMMITT

BE A COMPETITOR

LEARN TO BE A GREAT COMMUNICATOR

MAKE WINNING AN ATTITUDE

DISCIPLINE YOURSELF SO NO ONE ELSE HAS TO

PUT THE TEAM BEFORE YOURSELF

DON'T JUST WORK HARD, WORK SMART

MAKE HARD WORK YOUR PASSION

Pat Summitt™

In the end, the hard work
is what makes our team have
so much faith in itself.

Another simple matter of respect
is being on time. Lateness
sends a message that you're either
too careless, or too special to be
on time.

Offense sells tickets,
defense wins games, rebounding
wins championships.

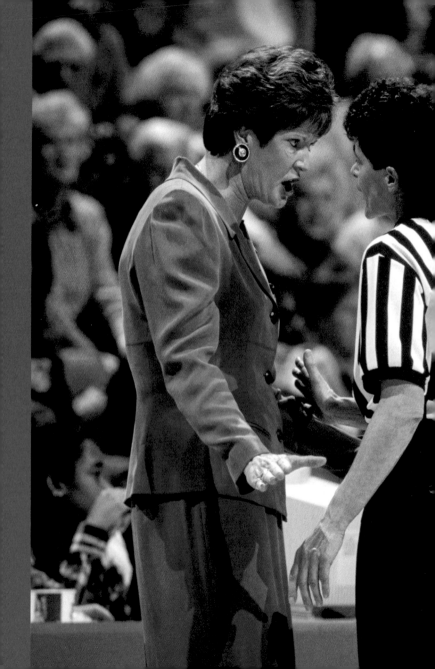

Pat Summitt™

Individual
success is a myth.
No one succeeds all by
themselves.

Pat Summitt™

RESPECT YOURSELF AND OTHERS

HANDLE SUCCESS LIKE YOU HANDLE FAILURE

TAKE FULL RESPONSIBILITY

CHANGE IS A MUST

DEVELOP AND DEMONSTRATE LOYALTY

BE A COMPETITOR

LEARN TO BE A GREAT COMMUNICATOR

MAKE WINNING AN ATTITUDE

DISCIPLINE YOURSELF SO NO ONE ELSE HAS TO

PUT THE TEAM BEFORE YOURSELF

MAKE HARD WORK YOUR PASSION

DON'T JUST WORK HARD, WORK SMART

THE DEFINITE DOZEN

12

BY PAT SUMMITT

Develop and demonstrate loyalty.

And when people participate
in setting their own goals,
standards and regulations they
tend to be more cooperative.

Discipline is not about the easy
solution. It's supposed to be thoughtful
and appropriate, not knee-jerk.
Remember, the purpose is to
train people (and yourself)
into good habits and out of bad ones.

Taking on too much can be
a morale breaker, and when morale
breaks down, so does self-discipline.

Pat Summitt

I love teaching both
the game and the
life skills accompanying it.
I have always said
the gym is
my classroom.

There is nothing wrong with
having competitive instincts.
They are survival instincts.

Make people accountable
for their piece of the puzzle.

Hard work is hard work.
The result of hard work is fun
and it is rewarding.

With a combination of practice
and belief, the most ordinary team
is capable of extraordinary things.

Why is communication important?
Because you can't do anything
without it.

Hard work breeds self-respect.

Pat Summitt

Discipline is the only sure way
I know to convince people
to believe in themselves.

▲▲

The trick to using
negative reinforcement is to
always phrase it as
a challenge.

▲▲

It's important to strike the right balance
between commending
and criticizing.

I won 1,098 games
and 8 national
championships, and
coached in four
different decades.
But what I see
are not the numbers.
I see their faces.

"Coaches of the Century"
UCLA's John Wooden
UT's Pat Summitt

Pat Summitt™

Responsibility never ends.
It's not a step or a chapter.
You don't finish it and
then move on to something
more fun or interesting.
Responsibility is a
constant state
of being.

Pat Summitt

Hard work is about
controlling those
things that you are
capable of controlling.

PatSummitt

Whatever it is that you
desire to do in life,
have the courage and
commitment to do it, and
do it at your
absolute best.

"Nobody walked off a college basketball court victorious more times than Pat Summitt. For four decades, she outworked her rivals, made winning an attitude, loved her players like family, and became a role model to millions of Americans, including our two daughters."
— *Barack Obama, Former President of the United States*

Recognitions

- Presidential Medal of Freedom
- Naismith Coach of the Century
- Honoring the "Coaches of the Century," the NCAA's Main Conference Room is The Pat Summitt – John Wooden Room
- Pat Summitt is the only woman author of the top 50 leadership books written by coaches
- Pat Summitt is the only woman on Sporting News' list of Top 50 U.S. Coaches of All Time, All Sports. Pat is listed #13.
- Received the John Bunn Award, the most prestigious award given by the Naismith Memorial Basketball Hall of Fame
- Named a "Twenty-Five Most Influential Working Mothers" by the White House
- Focus of an ESPN "30-By-30" feature film titled "Pat XO"
- U.S. News & World Report "Top 50 Women Leaders in the U.S."
- Sports Illustrated's "Sportswoman of the Year"
- Glamour Magazine's "Woman of the Year"
- Honorary Doctorate from U.S. Sports Academy
- Lifetime Achievement Award from The President's Council
- Arthur Ashe Courage Award from ESPN

"Pat meant a great deal to me. Pat was a great friend to me and a great resource. Even though I never played for her, I always felt like she was one of my coaches. I used to lean on her for advice. The words legend or icon are probably used too much in today's sports society. They are certainly appropriate, however, when describing Pat Summitt. That's what she was."
— *Peyton Manning, Tennessee All-American & NFL All-Pro Quarterback*